For further information about the path of Sant Mat, contact
Know Thyself as Soul Foundation:
Toll free: 1-877-MEDITATE   www.santmat.net

SIMRAN

The Sweet Remembrance of God

Kirpal Singh

*"Man's only duty is to be ever grateful to God
for His innumerable gifts and blessings."*

I have written books without any copyright—no rights reserved—because it is a Gift of God, given by God, as much as sunlight; other gifts of God are also free.

—from a talk by Kirpal Singh, with the author of a book after a talk to students of religion at Santa Clara University, San Jose, California on November 16, 1972.

The text of this book is the same as what was published during the lifetime of Master Kirpal Singh. Aside from punctuation and capitalization corrections, no changes have been made to the text; it is exactly the same as what was approved by Master Kirpal Singh.

First Edition, February 1954
Second Edition, May 1967
Third Edition, July 1971
This Edition published in 2010

RUHANI SATSANG®
DIVINE SCIENCE OF THE SOUL
250 "H" Street, #50
Blaine, WA 98230-4018 USA

www.RuhaniSatsangUSA.org
Tel: 1 (888) 530-1555

ISBN # 978-0-942735-08-6
SAN 854-1906

Printed in the United States of America
by Print Graphics Pros • (949) 859-3845

Sant Kirpal Singh Ji
(1894-1974)

*Dedicated
to the Almighty God
working through all Masters who have come
and Baba Sawan Singh Ji Maharaj
at whose lotus feet
the writer imbibed sweet elixir of
Holy Naam — the Word*

Sawan Singh Ji Maharaj

Sant Kirpal Singh passed on from this earth in 1974. Therefore, He is no longer taking on new people to guide out of this world and back to God. He left many books that explain, as much as can be conferrred in a worldly language, the meaning of life. The books and the Ruhani Satsang website http://www.Ruhani SatsangUSA.org/ are maintained to help stir an interest in God and to help people know what to look for in their search for the way back home.

When asked about a successor, we can only offer this quotation from the Master:

> *Today there is a great awakening beginning. Some have got the answer, some have not, but the search to solve the mystery of life has been born all over the world. The day that question arises in the mind is the greatest day of one's life, for once it is born, it does not succumb until it is satisfied.*
>
> *So, make your life an example of the teachings you follow — live up to them.*
>
> *If you have a strong desire to get it, then God Himself will make the arrangements for you.*

[Excerpts from a talk published in the January 1971 issue of *Sat Sandesh*]

Contents

Introduction 1

Simran 12

    The Seat of Simran 16

    The Basic Names of God 17

    How to Do Simran 20

    Kabir on Simran 24

Conclusion 38

List of Books by Kirpal Singh 45

Truth is higher than everything but higher still is true living. Truth and true living are not exclusive of each other but go together; one supplements the other and their combination forms the God-like life. One who practices true living will always earn his living by the sweat of his brow and feed himself and his family on rightly procured foods consisting of fruits, vegetables, nuts, cereals and permitted dairy products. Furthermore, he will be honest and aboveboard in his dealings with others.

INTRODUCTION

Dear Brothers and Sisters:

Mr. Khanna has asked me to give some message on my birthday anniversary. The day of my physical birth fell on the 6th of February, 1894. The true date of my birth is the day when I sat physically at the holy feet of my Master SAWAN SINGH, in February 1924. Still the truer date is when I was reborn anew into the beyond and met my Master in all His glory in 1917, i.e., seven years before my meeting with Him physically. I respect all holy scriptures of all the Saints who came in the past as all those were given by inspiration of God. I had the good fortune to sit at the feet of my Master. That which I have received of my Master, the same I deliver unto you. I find the same parallel with what all the past Saints have said. The difference is in the language or the way of expression, but the subject matter is the same. They all talk as to how to liberate our souls from mind and matter and know ourselves and know God. At the time of Initiation, Satguru resides with the devotee. He is with you always even unto the end of the world and will be extending all feasible help. He will never leave thee, nor forsake thee. Whosoever's mind is stayed on Him with full faith, He will keep him in perfect peace. There is hope for everybody. Master Power comes into the world to save sinners and to put them on the way back to God. It is for you to remain devoted to Him and keep His commandments. The rest is for Him to do. God is Love. You are also love. Love is the potent factor to meet God. He that loveth not, knoweth not God. Therefore, thou shalt love the Lord thy God with all thy heart and with all thy soul and with all thy mind. I wish you to be the doers of the Word and not hearers only, for an ounce of practice is worth more than tons of theories. Reformers are badly needed, not of others, but of themselves. You shall have Godhead as salary. I wish you all Godspeed in your efforts to tread the way back to God, which lies within you. My love and best wishes are always with you and will remain with you. The mystery of life is solved in the company of those who have solved that for themselves. How to find such a man? One who solved this mystery can help you in finding the same truth.

Someone questioned Guru Nanak as to how one could find a true and real Guru, and by what signs He could be recognized. Guru Nanak replied: "The human body is a temple of God, and it is by turning within that we meet God. There is a way from this house of the body to another house within (the Nij Ghar or Sach Khand) which is the Real House and here the soul finds everlasting peace. The human body is just like a rented house, given to us temporarily (i.e., allotted span of life) until, in the meanwhile, the soul is wise enough to gain access to her permanent abode of everlasting bliss. Now, the Real and True Master is one who can show us the way out to the Kingdom of God within this body and can lead the soul from stage to stage until the kingdom is gained and the soul comes into her own."

The human body, like any other physical thing, is subject to decay and disintegration. Even this world suffers dissolution. But Sach Khand or the Kingdom of God alone is indestructible and eternal. The process of Dissolution works up to the realm of the Triloki or three worlds (physical, astral and causal planes) and that of Grand Dissolution up to the subtlest of the causal planes; but it cannot reach Sach Khand, or Sat Lok, or Mukam-i-Haq as the Mohammedans call it (New Jerusalem of the Christians), for it is the veritable Kingdom of God, as spoken of by Christ. The Saints have, therefore, set Sach Khand as their goal, which is beyond the ken of Dissolution and Grand Dissolution.

Next, the Satguru or the True Master points out the way to the Kingdom of God. He tells us that the Divine Music comprised of five strains or melodies is always going on in the body. This continuous symphony is the connecting link between the Creation and the Creator. It is the ladder which the soul has to climb step by step in its onward journey to the Kingdom of God. This Music is most melodious, the like of which cannot be found on Earth. It has immense attraction and an irresistible appeal in it. The different melodies begin from Sahas dal Kanwal (the region of the thousand petaled lotus) and reach as far as Sach Khand. The Master Soul gives a contact to the human soul at the lowest end of the Musical notes, besides some experience of the withdrawal of the sensory current from the body, **both of which have to be developed by daily practice.**

The Satguru comes into the world with the treasure of Naam. The Muslims call it the Nada-i-Asmani (heavenly music) and Christians describe it as "Word." The treasure of Naam is not the heritage of this or that particular nation or community, nor of any particular country, nor of any religion, caste, or creed. Again, this treasure is freely distributed by a Master Soul to all, irrespective of any of the above considerations. An aspirant may be a Brahmin or Kshatriya, a Hindu or a Muslim, or anything else, for that is not of any consequence. Each one of us can learn The Art of Life and The Science of Spirituality so as to find a way out to the Kingdom of God which is the common heritage of all and the summum bonum of life.

Again, a Master Soul may come into the world in any garb He may choose. It is of no consequence to the aspirants for spirituality. Any such considerations will surely be a hindrance and a positive disadvantage. Our only connection with the Master Soul is purely of a spiritual nature and not a temporal one. Saint Kabir, though a Muslim weaver, had among His followers Rajput chieftains like Bir Singh and Bhaghail Singh. Similarly Saint Ravi Das, a cobbler by profession, had Mira Bai, a Rajput princess, and Raja Pipa in His sacred fold. All that we have to ascertain is that the Master is Shabda Sanehi. He who loves the Word is Word personified and can give us first hand experience of the Shabd or the Sound Principle to start with. If He satisfies these conditions, we should have no scruples on any ground whatsoever in accepting Him and learning from Him the Science of Spirituality.

The macrocosm is in the microcosm. The human body is the prototype of the universe and much more than that. In it there are millions of solar systems with their suns, moons, and earths revolving in and out. The sweetest of the sweet music is also going on in it, emanating from the true throne of the True King — God.

A Muslim divine also says in this respect: "When I heard the bewitching strains of that celestial song, Kaaba (the holiest of the holy places of Muslim worship) and the temple (of the idol worshippers) both appeared to be bad caricatures before the divine intoxication it gave."

Maulana Rumi says: "The Saints are the True Devotees of God, always listening to the Divine Music within. That infuses life into the lovers of God." Shamas Tabriz, another Muslim Saint, also speaks of it: "Every moment a strange type of call is coming from the Heaven. I hear that voice and none else. Blessed indeed are they who hear this call."

This song is quite unique in character. No language can describe it — neither Turkish, nor Arabic, nor Persian, nor any other. It is, in fact, an Unspoken Language and an Unwritten Law unto itself.

The Prophet Mohammed once declared that He listened to the Voice of God just as He listened to any other voice. But when questioned as to why it could not be heard by others, He said, '"You cannot hear this Voice as your ears have been sealed up. Hie to some Master Soul with a prayer for breaking of the seal and then listen attentively in the silence of your heart."

Mrs. Annie Besant, the great Theosophist, calls it the Voice of the Silence and says that the Silence becomes vocal when the mind is at perfect rest.

"The Kingdom of God is within you," says Christ. The trouble is that we search for it without and find it not. Man in his search for God has not spared any efforts. He has looked for Him in the sacred rivers (like Ganges, etc.), in the snow-capped mountains of Badrinath, Kailash, Amarnath, etc., in the deep recesses of the forests, and in the sacred places of all antiquity, but with no success. As the "way out" to God lies within, you will have to find a Master who knows the Way and would be a guide unto you until the goal is reached. This work only a True Master can do and no one else can do it.

Now the question comes: Where can this Divine Music be contacted? To this the Master replies, "This Divine Music is going on in Sukhmana (a central cord between Ida and Pingala, the two cords on either side, which running through the spine and passing through the center of and between the two eyebrows, reaches directly as far as Sach Khand or Shah Rag as named by the Muslims). It can be experienced by the soul in her deepest depths, when layer by layer the various sheaths or coverings (physical or gross, mental or subtle, and causal) are shaken off from the soul in her onward journey to the various Lokas or regions: the sun, the moon, the stars, of spirits (Pithrian), of Deities (Devian), etc. At each stage, the Music becomes more enrapturing than before, until in Par Brahm (beyond the three Lokas) the soul becomes self-luminous in her pristine glory; then the Music, too, becomes exceedingly charming, in full swell with unending continuity. This is the Ajapa Jap going on at all times in an Unspoken Language. As the soul hears it she gets magnetized, with the result that the mind with its outgoing faculties is paralyzed for want of the inspiration it is used to drawing from the Spirit, and gradually it loses its hold of her. The high-born maiden (being a drop of the ocean of Sat Nam) is freed from its clutches and now moves on unhampered."

It is, of course, impossible to describe the sublime symphonies in so many words, as they are past description for want of adequate expression.

At present every soul has, on account of constant association with mind, acquired a tendency to flow downward and outward through the outgoing faculties. It is because of this that she cannot catch the Sound Current (the Elixir of Life) within. A cup turned upside down may for ages remain in the rain, but not a drop will fall into it. But if it is turned aright, it will get filled up in one or two showers. Exactly is it the case with the soul. As soon as the Master Soul gives her a contact with the life-giving Sound Current, by turning it aright through the withdrawal of the sensory current, the lotus-like cup of the spirit gets more and more water of Immortality until she gets drenched through and through and is saved forever.

Mind, you know, is ever after pleasures of one kind or another. But the pleasures of this world are all transitory and have always some sting at the bottom. "Our sincerest laughter with some pain is fraught," says an English poet.

This renegade of the mind can only be subdued if some internal pleasure of rapturous strains of the Divine Music — the Word — is given to it in lieu of the external one. When mind tastes the sweet Elixir, it is diverted from the worldly enjoyments and is subdued. The soul becomes free. This is the only remedy by which the sages controlled the mind. It held good in all ages — the Golden, the Silver and the Copper, and holds good even today in Kali Yuga or the Iron Age. The Sat is eternal. It was in the beginning. It was in the middle, and it shall ever remain until Eternity. The Divine Music of Sat is then the sovereign remedy for stilling the mind. In due course of time, by regular practice, the soul becomes fully absorbed into the Elixir of Naam, and the mind is rendered absolutely ineffectual.

As said above, the Sound Current begins from Turya Pad when, the sensory current having withdrawn from the body, the soul enters into the Beyond. The five strains in seriatim follow one another from one spiritual plane to another until Sach Khand is reached. One has to take hold of each of these strains or melodies for traversing from stage to stage until the final stage is attained. It is only here that salvation of the soul is assured and the cycle of births and deaths ends. This is the grand purpose of life, which one fulfills through the grace of the Master Soul.

The Master Saint Shamas Tabriz says: "The Great God has turned us out and closed strongly the door behind the eyes. He Himself comes to us in the garb of a man to take us back into His fold."

The method by which He lets us in once again is explained further:

First one has to withdraw into the silence of the soul, before he begins to hear the five strains of Music. The sensory current is to be withdrawn at the seat of the soul behind the eyebrows. The journey onward begins from this stage, the seventh in the order from below. When the soul rises above the six chakras or ganglions in the Pind or physical body and starts toward Sahans dal Kanwal (thousand petaled lotus), the seventh stage, she catches the first of the five strains of the Divine Music and proceeds further. There is no Naam in the lower six chakras. These, in fact, are the grave, from which we have to rise above and come to the point from where the Grand Trunk Road of Spirituality begins.

Another Saint says, "At the seventh stage you begin to hear the five strains of the Divine Music, when you remove the tent of the soul from the graveyard of the body comprising the six lower chakras. From here heavenly Music takes charge of the soul and pulls it up from stage to stage until the final consummation with Sat Purush or Sat Naam takes place."

Almost all the Saints have given the same qualifications of a True Master. Guru Arjan says, "Accept that man as a Guru who can give you an experience of the Truth, the Naam. That is indescribable, no doubt, but we must have some contact thereof." In short, whoever can tune us into the Shabd — the Divine Music. Kabir also speaks in the same terms: "We have so many sadhus, the great ones. I have respect for all of them. But the one who is One with the Word, and can give us a contact with that, He overtops all; and I have the greatest regard for Him." Swami Shiv Dayal Singh Ji also speaks in the same way: "Guru is He who has love of Shabd and practices no other methods except that. Whoever practices Shabd is the perfect Guru. You sit at His feet, who will give you a contact with it." He who is Word Personified, who was Word made flesh and dwelt amongst us, and can give us a contact with that, is held in high esteem by all Saints. The Holy Scriptures all speak in volumes of their greatness.

It is through the grace of God alone that a jiva (soul) comes across such a Master Soul or Guide who is well versed in the science of Surat Shabd Yoga. The Master in extreme compassion takes him into His fold and links him up with the Sound Current and thereby puts him on the path of final liberation. Guru Nanak says that he is an admirer of the man who reaches his true home in this way.

The course of Surat Shabd Yoga, as described by Guru Nanak, is the most natural one. It can be practiced by man or woman, young or old, alike. Even a child can practice it with ease. It is designed by God Himself and not by any human agency, and therefore it admits of no addition, alteration or modification.

It is God's Law that nobody can reach Him except through a Master Soul. This is what is given out by almost all the Saints who came so far.

The Master teaches us how to withdraw from the body and contact the Sound Current — the Word within. There are so many ways to withdraw from the body but the one devised by the Saints is most natural and quickest and **that is achieved through SIMRAN or repetition of the names of God.** So I would like to just give in detail something about this subject which is very important and is the first step toward going up. As far as the Word or Naam is concerned I have already given a talk separately. I will now speak on Simran.

SIMRAN

Everyone in the world is doing Simran of one kind or another. In fact none can do without it. A housewife, for instance, is thinking all the while of the kitchen requirements like flour, pulses, spices and pepper, lest any of these things run short. She is thinking of recipes for new dishes and delicacies. Similarly, a farmer is always thinking of ploughing the land, furrowing the fields, sowing the seeds and harvesting and the like, besides his cattle and fodder. A shopkeeper is preoccupied with his stock-in-trade and keenly alive to rise and fall in the prices of commodities he deals in, and how he can make huge profits in his business. A schoolmaster, likewise, dreams of his school, classes, pupils and lessons, on all of which his attention is closely riveted. Again a contractor is engrossed in problems of labor, material, and various building processes.

Thus, everyone of us is constantly dwelling on one thing or another. This close association leaves an imprint in the human mind which, in course of time, becomes indelible enough and leads to complete identification of the subject with the object — and hence it is said, "As you think so you become," or "Where the mind is there you are also," no matter where the physical self is. This being the case, Saints take hold of a person from the line of least resistance.

As no one can do without Simran, the Saints try to set one type of Simran for another type. They substitute for Simran of the world and worldly relations and objects, a Simran of God's Name, or "Word." As the former leads to distraction of the mind, the latter pulls heavenward, leading to peace of mind and liberation of the soul. Three to four hours in a day has been enjoined as the minimum for Simran, and it may be gradually increased. The Mahatmas are never without Simran even for a single moment. As it is altogether a mental process (for it is to be done by the tongue of thought), no amount of physical and manual labor can interfere with it. In course of time, like the tick of a clock, it becomes automatic and ceaseless for all the twenty-four hours. While the hands are engaged in work, the mind rests in the Lord.

I now give you some details of recipes prescribed for doing Simran or repetition of the Name of God.

All persons are engaged in the doing of Simran in one form or another. Some do Simran by means of a beaded string called a rosary. In this type of Simran one cannot maintain undivided attention, for while doing it one has to roll off the beads with his fingers and reverse the head-knot on completion of each round of the rosary. In this way one cannot have single-minded devotion, without which there can be no gain. By constant practice the fingers automatically roll over the beads while the unbridled mind keeps wandering astray. This is why Master Souls always lay emphasis on mental Simran or one that is done with the tongue of thought. For Simran done with concentrated attention alone is beneficial.

Again, there are persons who do Simran with their

tongue. This type of Simran, too, is no better than that done with the help of the rosary. In this type also the tongue wags on in the mouth, while the mind runs riot all the time.

Some do Simran at the seat of the thyroid gland. This as well does not count for much unless it is done with attention fully riveted to it.

Still others do Simran at the seat of the heart in unison with the constant heart beat, but here again sine qua non is whole-hearted attention before one can expect any benefit from it. Another type of Simran is one that is done with the breath vibration of the vital air as it goes in and comes out; it gives just temporary stillness and is of little value.

Each of the above Sadhans (practices) has more efficacy in ascending order than the one preceding, but none of them per se is efficacious enough unless it is done with undivided attention. A person may experience a little calm for a while, but it cannot help the spirit in withdrawal and concentration at the seat of the soul just behind the center of the two eyebrows.

The Master Souls in all times and in all climes have, therefore, gone to the very root of the thing — the discovery of the self called Atma-Siddhi, the experience of the Changeless One, beyond time, space and causation — something subtler, higher, nobler, purer and more powerful in the entire creation, and have enjoined Simran of the Highest Order: one done mentally on the Divine Ground, before the threshold of God's own door, about which Christ says, "Knock and it shall be opened unto thee." Again the gospel says with regard to single-minded attention, "If thine eye be single, thy whole body shall be filled with light." This eye is called in Sanskrit as Shiv-Netra or Dev-drishti. The Muslims describe it as Nukta-i-Sweda. William Wordsworth, a great romantic poet, refers to it as an "Inward Eye."

Muslim Saints classify Simran or Zikr into five categories:

1. Zikr-i-Lassani or Zikr done with the tongue. It is also called Kalma-e-Shariet or Nasut.

2. Zikr-i-Qalbi, done with Qalb or at the seat of the heart by the process of Habas-i-dam (Pranayam or control of the breath). It is technically called Kalma-i-Tariqat or Malqut.

3. Zikr-i-Ruhi, done with full attention and known as Kalma-i-Marefat or Jabrut.

4. Zikr-i-Siri, that leads to the inn or secret of reality. It is named Kalma-i-Haqiqat or Lahut.

5. Lastly Zikr-i-Khaffi, or one that unlocks the secret door. It is called Hahut.

Maulana Rumi, a Muslim Saint, while speaking of Zikr or Simran, therefore considers such Zikr alone of the highest type as helps in manifesting the Reality within, viz., Zikr-i-Ruhi as opposed to Zikr-i-Lassani.

Similarly Rishi Sandilya in His Upanishad tells us that Bekhri Simran (done with the tongue) is quite good, but Upasu (done with the breath slowly) is better still, while Manski (done mentally with the tongue of thought) is the best and tops all the rest.

The Seat of Simran:

Now we have to see where the repetition of Naam is to be done.

The Divine Ground on which Simran should be done is the center between the two eyebrows called variously as Third Eye, Tisra Til, Shiv-Netra or Mukta-i-Sweda. It is the gateway leading to the subtle planes. In the state of wakefulness it is the seat of the spirit or psyche, and it is located above the six physical ganglions. We have to transcend both the astral and causal planes above the physical plane. The Yogis, step by step, cross over the six physical centers until they finally and completely traverse and go over the physical plane. Instead of descending down into the lower ganglions and then going up by piercing them through in the upward journey, it would be easier and better by far if one were to commence the journey right ahead from the seat of the soul in the wakeful state which is at the back of the two eyes. The easiest way to withdraw the spirit from the body to its own seat is by means of some mental Simran, as may be enjoined by the Master Soul.

The Basic Names of God:

Let us now see what Simran is and what the relation is between the Name and named.

For Simran there are two kinds of Names, original and derivative. Generally people engage in Simran of one or another of the derivative or attributive Names of God, as may have an appeal to the individual concerned. This may be good and useful to a certain extent, but it cannot work as an "Open Sesame" to the higher spiritual planes within.

Master Souls always do and recommend Simran of the highest type, to wit, of the Original or **Basic Names of God** for these open up charmed casements and bring to view vistas leading to spiritual realms within the body. Such Names are charged with and electrified by the thought transference that usually accompanies them when communicated to an aspirant by a Master Soul. As these are magnetized, they have the power to attract and pull the spirit up to the planes to which they relate. The engrafted "Words" charged with the Divine Spirit of the Master very soon bear fruit. Christ in this connection says, "I am the vine, ye are the branches, and as branches cannot do without the vine, ye cannot do without me ... Let you abide in me and my words abide in you."

Again, these charmed words of the Master — Basic Names of God — have the power to dispel the forces of darkness that may meet and assail a Spirit on its onward journey. Simran of these names helps the soul both in the physical plane and supra-physical plane, one after the other. Hence it is imperative that Simran be done of such Names as the Master-Soul enjoins, for they are charged with a tremendous spiritual power which negative powers can hardly put up with, and from which they flee as from an enchanter driven. Immortal and everlasting as these words of the Master are, they bestow life everlasting to the soul in which they sink and take root. Death cannot come near such a soul. This is why it is said, "Take not God's name in vain."

Every name has its own significance, influence, energy, and power. If one thinks of ice, he is reminded of the bleak cold and the shivers it brings; the thought of fire puts into mind its attributes of heat and warmth. The word "lawyer" is suggestive of courts and cases, and "doctor" at once conjures up pictures of hospitals, patients and medicinal chests, etc. It is a common saying, "As you think so you become." Thought is said to be the keynote to success. There is always a strong link between a name and the named, and much greater and stronger is this link between God and His Names. It may be said that God Himself resides and dwells in His own Names (basic and original and not derivative or attributive).

Simran of the Basic Names of God has an inevitable influence on the mind. It leads to dhyan, making the spirit forgetful of the world and worldly objects. In meditation nothing but concentrated Simran remains; and from the great and deep silence of the heart (Hriday Kamal of the Saints, i.e., the Divine

Ground behind the eyebrows), there issues forth a ceaseless Sound Current, which helps in pulling the spirit up, leading to the withdrawal from the body (without, of course, breaking the silver chord) and guides the spirit in its onward journey into various spirit realms. The luminous form of the Master always remains with the spirit, helping and guiding it at every step. **This Sound Principle is the link between God and man,** and in this way an indissoluble bond and relationship is established between the Creator and His creation. This Sound Current is variously described by various sages. The Vedas speak of it as Sruti (that which is heard) the Upanishads describe it as Nad or Udgit (song of the other world). The Muslims call it as Bang-i-Asmani or Kalma. In Gurbani we have references to Shabd and in the Gospel it is mentioned as the Word. The Zoroastrians call it Sarosha and the French have given It the name of Elan-vital or life current.

Once the consciousness takes root in this Sound Principle or Voice of the Silence, life everlasting is assured to the spirit. There is no other way to God than this, and it can be reached only by means of Simran of God's Names. "Knock and it shall be opened unto thee" is what the Gospel preached. Emerson calls it "tapping inside." This knocking and tapping is possible only when through Simran the mind is stilled and the spirit is withdrawn and concentrated before the very door of God. This then is the way as ordained by God Himself; but no one can find it without the grace of the Master Soul, an adept in the

Science of Spirituality, not only in theory like Yog Valik, but in practice as well like Ashtavakra, one who has transcended all the planes (physical, subtle, causal and beyond) and holds commission from God to lead other souls to Him.

How to Do Simran:

For Simran one has to adopt some convenient posture and then to fix his attention on the Divine Ground between the eyebrows. Simran is entirely a mental process and is to be done mentally with the tongue of thought, while the gazing faculty is to be fixed at the spot behind the two eyebrows as said above. The Words, as given by the Master, may slowly be repeated mentally or with the tongue of thought. It should be done without causing any strain or pressure on the forehead. The practice may be started with a half hour or so as may be convenient, but in course of time it should be developed to two or three hours a day or even longer. Simran of the Divine Names introverts the mind and weans it from worldly thoughts and mundane matters, until it gets stilled and is equipoised.

Some do Simran with closed eyes and others with open eyes. The first, in some cases, sinks into drowsiness leading to what may be called Yog Nidra; and the second, in some cases, keeps the mind engaged on environments. One has, therefore, to guard against both pitfalls. Simran with closed eyes is preferable provided one retains full consciousness. It must be done regularly every day at a fixed time. Hafiz, a

Sufi poet of Persia, says, "The only job is to pray, unmindful of whether the same is accepted or not." This means you have to remember the Lord internally without any clutching nature or receiving one thing or the other. We have to leave everything to Lord or Master working overhead. Just as we need food for the body, so do we need food for the soul. We are very careful in giving food to the horse of the body, but starve the rider — the spirit — the life-giving fountainhead that enlivens the body and without which it has no value. We must provide food to spirit more regularly and timely than we do for the body, no matter where we are, whether at home or abroad, and no matter what the circumstances may be, this should be our first and foremost concern.

The Simran of Naam or Word is an elixir of life and, in fact, a panacea (healing) for all ills, physical, mental, accidental or ordained. It is a food for the spirit; and when the spirit is strong and healthy, it will charge the body with vital currents of life and light (elan vital) dispelling all darkness from head to foot. It is the Bread of Life spoken of by Christ when He declared you cannot live on bread alone. **But you can live on the Name of God alone.**

Simran and Dhyan (meditation) flood the spirit with the waters of life. Spirit comes to its own, rises in its latent Godhood and, like a tumultuous mountain stream, rushes headlong toward the ocean of life which is its perennial source and merges therein losing its separate identity.

There are no limitations as to time and place for Simran. It may be done at any time and at any place, sitting or standing, walking, or in bed; but it must be done in a state of conscious wakefulness. Early morning hours (Amrit Vela) is the best time for Simran. A light and frugal night meal consisting of milk and fruits and morning ablutions are aids in the right direction. Purity of thoughts, words, and deeds go a long way to make a success of the Sadhan (spiritual discipline), for ethical life precedes spiritual life and is, in fact, the very ground on which the spiritual structure has to be raised. For a householder, it is very necessary to observe strict discipline in life in matters of diet, drink, and speech. Again Simran must be done slowly and the Words are to be repeated or thought out with clarity. The whole process is to be carried out with love, devotion, and single-minded attention to ensure quick results. When properly done for some time, a state of divine intoxication comes upon the spirit and blessed calmness is experienced. All worldly thoughts vanish like thin air and the spirit feels freed from the bodily tenements and is irresistibly drawn upward by the Unseen Power of the Master. When it thus withdraws from the sensual planes, it gets concentrated at its own seat; the inner light dawns, and one by one spiritual experiences like starry welkin, the moon and the sun unfold themselves. One comes across frequent references to these things in all the scriptures, both ancient and modern, like the Vedas, the Upanishads, the Holy Koran, the Gurbani, the Gospel, etc. The Prophets Mohammed and Moses speak of the various inner lights. In the Gospel there are repeated references to the thunder and lightning in connection with the Voice of God as it spoke to the prophets.

As the spirit crosses over these initial stages and lands in the subtle plane, the luminous form of the Master appears, takes charge of the soul, and leads it on the onward spiritual journey from plane to plane. With the advent of the Master, the work of Simran is completed, and the aspirant soul lies wholly in the hands of the Master Soul.

Guru Arjan, the fifth Guru of the Sikhs, has given a glowing account of the results which a man can have by doing the sweet remembrance of the Word. He impresses on the man to remember Him all the time in so many words as used by the Saints in the past. There are so many names of the One Reality, and our aim and goal is common. **We have to start from the name and contact with the Named.** Unless you contact the Named you cannot derive the full benefit of the words repeated by you. For instance, you say "water" in English, "aqua" in Latin, "pani" and "ash" in Urdu and Persian, "jal" and "nir" in Hindi; but by repetition of these names alone, your thirst cannot be satisfied. It is only by drinking the particular fluid which is called by so many names that your thirst is appeased. By doing Simran of the world and its environments, they have so much taken possession of us that we have become the world and its environments. We have to use the same methods, so as to eliminate all the worldly thoughts from within, by remembering sweetly of the Lord in so many words devised by the Saints so far. So there are two uses of Simran: one use is to withdraw from the body by Simran of the electrified words given by a competent Master, and the second is to drive out the world and its thoughts from within us by the constant remembrance of the Lord in so many ways as prescribed, the description of which has been given above in detail.

Kabir on Simran:

I have given a digest of the whole subject matter in connection with Simran. It will not be out of place to put before you the sayings of the different Saints on this subject. I now put before you the statements made by Saint Kabir on the subject. He says: "Comforting is God's Name. All ills it dries (cures). Remembrance of God's Name leads to Him besides." Further, Kabir says: "Amongst high love, 'mongst rich and poor, Great is he who prays and greater still he that motiveless does so."

The pelf and power hardly make a man. Poverty and riches are both transitory. A man of Simran stands far above all mankind. He is much more blessed than the rest. Most people crave for worldly things. Some are desirous of having children, others hanker after wealth, and still others after name and fame. The kind Father, of course, grants prayers of all. But a man of Simran, on the other hand, asks for nothing. He seeks God for God's sake and hence is the crowning glory to Him.

Once Akbar, the great Moghul Emperor, while riding lost his way and felt thirsty. He asked a farmer standing near a well for water. The peasant tied the Emperor's horse to a nearby tree and gave water and food to him, little knowing who he was. The King was pleased with his hospitality and told him who he was and bade the farmer to see him, should he ever stand in need of anything. After some time the farmer had an opportunity to visit the metropolis. He went to see the King as he was bidden to do so. On going to the royal palace, he found that the King was busy praying, and at the end he requested God for the peace and prosperity of his kingdom. Seeing this, the farmer felt humiliated for having come to beg from a beggar; for he, too, could directly appeal to the Great God, who listens alike to the prayers of both rich and poor.

Guru Nanak has said, "Why should we ask for worldly things from God?" All those who love the body and bodily relations go the way of hell, but one who does Simran motiveless is truly great. We generally pray for the fulfilment of our wishes and desires. So long as a man or a woman is full of these, the human body, far from being a temple of God, is an abode of Satan. So Kabir says that God loves those who love God alone: for no other purpose but for the love of God. The same is in the Sikh Scriptures: "What should I ask for? There is nothing lasting in all the world over. I see the whole world passing away."

Kabir says, "In pain we pray to God; in pleasure

we forget; Could we in pleasure pray, then pain would not come up."

We remember God only when we are hard pressed from every side. It is affliction and not affluence that turns us God-ward. If one were not to forget God in prosperity, adversity will never come near him. Hard times only come as a result of sins committed when forgetful of the Lord. Simran (or constant remembrance of God) is a tonic for the soul. It makes the will grow stronger from day to day. Troubles and trials however severe cannot cow him down. With a smiling face he pulls through the storms of fate or destiny unscathed. Simran is a panacea for all the ills of the world. It is a potent remedy and works wonders to remove worry where all human efforts fail. A man of Simran never has any worry or anxiety.

Simran, to be very effective, must be constant and ceaseless. Once Moses, the Prophet of the Hebrews, felt that he was the most devoted of God's creatures. In an egotistic frame of mind, he questioned God if there was in the world a devotee greater than himself. The Great God told Moses that among His devotees were included many birds, and animals besides human beings. Pointing to a solitary bird in the jungle, God directed Moses to meet the said bird, if he wanted to know the great depths of devotion. As Moses did not know the language of the birds, God endowed him with an understanding so that he may have a talk with the bird. Moses approached the bird and inquired as to how he was. The bird replied that engaged as he was in constant remembrance (Simran), he could ill afford any time for a useless conversation, except for the Beloved's sake who had sent Moses to him. Next, the prophet asked the bird if he had any trouble in which he could be of any help to him. The bird replied that he had no trouble whatsoever; but if the prophet wished to do him a favor, he asked him to bring nearer to him the spring of water that lay at a distance, as a flight to it to quench his thirst interfered in his Simran. This incident humbled the pride of Moses.

Guru Nanak also speaks in this wise: "If I forget You, O God, even for a fraction of a minute, this amounts to me more than fifty years." Again He says, "He who is in constant remembrance of God, only he is alive, O Nanak; all others are as it were dead."

Simran must be done at all costs. Constant remembrance of God is life-giving to the devotee. Guru Nanak says, "If I remember Thee I live. When I forget thee that means death to me." There are many devices to develop concentration. Some stand for hours and hours. Others keep their arms uplifted. Some engage in breathing exercises like Pranayam, and some sleep on nails or sit under the burning sun with four fires lit around them (i.e., Panch Agni Tap or the austerity of the five fires). But all these methods are artificial. Simran or the remembrance of God is the only natural method and the easiest to follow and develop. It can be practiced with equal ease by both the young and the old — in one's hearth and home, and in the midst of kith and kin, as well as in his business.

Kabir further says: "Forgetful of prayer in pleasure, we pray only in pain, so says Kabir, such prayers go all in vain."

Since we remember the Lord only when in trouble and never care for Him when in affluent circumstances, Saint Kabir says that God also does not listen to such selfish prayers which are muttered in vain in distress over one's ailments, or when one is involved in a lawsuit, etc.

Prayer should be ceaseless, overflowing as a lover's passions are, forgetting not his love even for the twinkling of an eye. When a man falls in love with a woman, he carries her image in his mind at all times whether sleeping or awake, sitting or standing. **If one could carry with him the love of God like this, it would be grand indeed.**

Kabir goes on to explain how the sweet remembrance of God should be done. He gives another example of the same type. He says, "Attend to the prayer as do the village maids, who move talking with attention always fixed on pitchers overhead."

The daily routine of life, says Kabir, does not interfere with the Simran. The village maids, as they go to fetch water, carry pitchers of water one above the other on their heads; and in spite of an unseen path, they keep jesting and talking among themselves while the pitchers remain steady on their heads, as their attention is pertinently fixed on them. Similarly one need not forget Simran even in the midst of the hustle and bustle of life and worldly obligations.

Kabir again says, "Attend to prayer as kine do the calves, Who grazing on the lea never forget their young."

When a grazier takes the cows for grazing, they do not forget the young ones they leave behind at home. All the while they are busy grazing in the field their attention remains fixed on their calves. In this way while engaged in worldly pursuits, we should not forget our aim and objective in life, i.e., God Realization.

Kabir gives another example to explain and bring home the fact that we should do the remembrance of the Lord. "Attend to the prayers as misers do the wealth, With mind forever fixed on the hoarded pelf."

A pauper collects his money by begging coppers and keeps counting the same day and night. Whether sleeping or waking, he is dreaming all the time of his little hoarding. We, too, should like a pauper always keep an account of the Simran that we do and try to accumulate bit by bit the wealth of Naam — not forgetting it for a moment.

Kabir has given so many examples so that we may understand the true value of real Simran which brings forth fruit.

"Love the prayer as the deer loves the trumpet sound

Who life and freedom risketh for sweet music's sake."

A fleet-footed deer, which cannot otherwise be caught, is entrapped by the hunters just by means of playing upon the trumpet. He is so enamoured of the sound that he is irresistibly drawn toward it and helplessly places his head on the musical instrument. In just the same way, when once the ever restless mind hears the Nad (or the Sound Current within) it is charmed, stilled, and becomes motionless. Soul, when freed from the tentacles or talons of the mind, is able to soar easily to higher regions.

Another example He gives: "Love the prayer as the moth loves the light; In its flame doth burn itself, never turns aside."

Light is the very life of the moth. He loves it so passionately that he does not hesitate to singe himself to death rather than to avoid it. Kabir Sahib therefore says that we must love Simran as the very breath of our life whether rich or poor, healthy or sick, awake or asleep and like a moth be ever ready to sacrifice our very self in our devotion to our ideal.

Again He says: "Lose yourself in the sweet remembrance as the insect doth bhirangi, who for sooth loses itself to rise bhirangi like."

Bhirangi (an insect) after almost killing a keet (another insect) revivifies the latter to life by bestowing its powerful attention to it. The keet when charmed back to life is no longer a keet, but becomes a bhirangi-being saturated with the life impulse of the latter. In just the same way Kabir says that one who does Simran and gets firmly engrafted therein will have new birth and a new life quite distinct from the old sensual life he has been living hitherto.

This is the "second birth" of which all the Saints speak. Christ says, "Unless you lose this life you cannot have life everlasting." "Except a man be born of water (first birth) and of the Spirit (second birth) he cannot enter the Kingdom of God." "The first birth was of corruptible seed, and the second shall be of seed incorruptible." This may be called *"birth in Christ";* and when it actually takes place, one would like St. Paul say, "It is not I but Christ speaks in me." The principle of engrafted life works alike in plants as well as in man and is in accord with the laws of Nature.

Hazrat Baziad Bustanvi, a man of extreme piety and devotion, once looked within himself and found nothing but God. In a state of divine intoxication he exclaimed, "I am God!" His disciples, unused to hearing such apparently sacrilegious words, wondered what had happened to the Pir (Master). After some time, when the Master had come down from the super-conscious state, they inquired of him why he had exclaimed that he was God which was quite contrary to his usual instructions to them (that God could not come into a human body). The Master told them that the expression "I am God" was not uttered by him, but by someone else (he could according to the Koranic Law be condemned as a heretic for uttering such blasphemous words). After some time, this Hazrat was once again seized by a fit of God intoxication and began to exclaim, "I am God." This time some of his disciples came down upon their Master with staves, spears, and swords. In the Maulana Masnavi, by Maulana Rumi (the original poetical narrative in this behalf), it is stated that whoever aimed a blow at the Master's head, hands, or legs got his own chopped off, while the Master beside himself kept chanting, "I am God." The disciples were amazed and inquired of the Pir the significance of the incident. The Pir with a smile on his face informed them, that one who merged his little entity (soul) into the greater entity (Oversoul) becomes One with God and no one could hit or harm him.

Similarly it is mentioned in Ghat Ramayan (a sacred book of the Hindus) that Tulsi Sahib of Hathras (a man of great devotion) when staying with Baji Rao Hulkar, a Maharatta chieftain of Stara, once said: "While the people see my physical raiment (the body), I actually live out of it."

Our own Master Hazur Baba Sawan Singh Ji was once on tour to Gujranwala city in the Punjab when some opponents came up with the idea of fighting. Master was inside. He rose up. He was in a state of God intoxication and said, "Look at me, who am I?" And it was all quiet.

This is the general experience of those who sometimes become God intoxicated. Such statements bring out the true meaning of Simran.

Saint Kabir gives so many examples. He says: "Love the prayer as fish love the water, who rather die than be separated from their element."

Water is the vital element of fish, without which they cannot live. A fish would prefer to die than live without it even for a single moment. Similarly, Simran (the Sound Current) is the vital element in which we live and move and have our being. Unless we by actual practice realize this fundamental truth, we cannot have peace.

Now He further explains: "Pray we with all our heart in the silence of the soul; Shut off the world without to unveil the Truth within."

Simran is to be done with the tongue of thought and not by word of mouth. It is entirely an inner mental process, to be practiced only after the outlets of the outgoing faculties are closed up.

The treasure of Simran is to be kept hidden from the people of the world. It is the most precious wealth, the value of which worldly people can hardly realize. **The reality dawns only when you tap the veil behind the eyes.** Christ, too, says in this behalf, "Seek and ye shall find. Knock and it shall be opened unto you."

Referring to the outer process which we generally do by way of Simran, Kabir says, "By telling beads we please ourselves and yet we never gain; But if we were to make a bead of the mind, an inward light would dawn again."

The telling of beads on the rosary gives just a mental satisfaction but leads nowhere. If you were to turn the beads of the mind, you would witness God's light within.

Kabir Sahib says that there is hardly any need of beaded rosaries, for while the hands are engaged in telling the beads, the mind is fixed on the beads without and cannot possibly withdraw within; and without this there is no gain whatsoever. Conversely, when the mind is once absorbed in Simran (mental concentration), the iron curtain will fling open (at the "Open Sesame" or enchanted words).

He says, "Aeons have passed in telling beads, yet our minds changed not; So cast off the wooden beads and take to the mental ones."

Kabir Sahib therefore says that we waste our entire life in performance of outer works of merits, but the soul finds no inlet. The veil within does not give way and soul remains without. We should, therefore, turn the bead of the mind; and it will act like a push-button giving an ingress of the soul to spiritual realms within."

Kabir further explains, "Continuous flow the symphonic strains sublime: Divine in birth, they subdue the mind."

By concentration, a feeling of numbness gradually creeps up on the hands and feet and spreads on to the rest of the body until the sensory current gets focused on the center of the soul behind the two eyebrows (from whence during wakefulness it proceeds). The concentrated energy then falls back upon the veil behind the eyes which is rent asunder, opening a brilliant vista ahead. The sun and the moon, in turn, appear with a melodious Sound Current emerging from beyond. These unbroken strains of music continue of their own accord. When this stage is reached an aspirant has nothing more to do except to be absorbed in them.

Kabir goes on further saying that: "True rosary lies in the mind, the rest is all sham and a worldly show; Lo, the rosary on the Persian wheel draws water alone."

Simran, to be effective, should be characterized by love, affection, and devotion. If the rosary alone were to lead to God, then the big rosary on the Persian wheel could, as well, do the same thing. But our daily experience shows that they fail to achieve any such thing (rosaries on the Persian wheel are the ropes to which the water pots are attached, and they fetch water only and nothing else).

Similarly, the Chinese have invented what is called the "Wheel of Prayer." If it is once put in motion it makes about a thousand rounds. They transcribe a mantra or a holy hymn on a piece of paper and put it on the wheel and set it into motion and feel satisfied that they have repeated the holy name a thousand times — but to no avail. Simran done parrot-like by repeating a mantra thousands of times in this way cannot bear any fruit.

Among orthodox Hindus there is a practice of writing the word "Ram, Ram" or the Word of God on paper in thousands every day. After some time they scissor down each word "Ram" and put it in a pill of flour and consign the said pills to the waters of some running stream, and believe that they have gained religious merit. It gives only a little remembrance of Ram. If one were to tell them that real Ram is within them, they would not believe it. So they neither find Ram nor do they get any substantial thing.

Similarly, Purbias (an orthodox sect who attach great importance to outer rituals and try to perform the same with religious faith) generally take a bath early in the morning in the waters of a running stream, as an act of religious merit. Once a few Purbias went to Kabul in Afghanistan (a hilly country to the northeast of India) where the weather is generally very cold. Here one of them went for a bath in the Kabul River, but finding the water icy cold, he hesitated to enter the stream. He thought of a good device to escape the ordeal and yet satisfy his scruples. He took up a pebble and threw it into the stream, saying, "O pebble, thy bath shall also be mine." After saying this he turned back and in the way met another Purbia going to the river for his morning ablutions. The latter asked him if he had taken the bath in the chilly bleak weather. The former informed him of the vicarious pebble-bath that he had had, and thereupon the other fellow embraced him saying, "Your bath is my bath as well." In this, blind leads the blind and both fall into the ditch by performing deeds blindly.

Kabir Sahib further refers to the rosary, saying: "Over the wooden rosary you have wasted much time; Now to the mental rosary take, that hath no knot on the end."

"O Kabir, the telling of the wooden-beaded rosary is a great laborious task, but continuous mental rosary, as of the breath beads (incoming and outgoing) is a natural phenomenon. It goes on endlessly without any effort."

In the rosary there is the head knot. When one round is completed, it is to be reversed so as not to neutralize the effect, for beads are to be told in one direction only. So Kabir advises that we should take to the natural rosary of the breath which, being endless continuation, has no knots and needs no reversal at all.

Further He says, "On continuous fruitless revolution, rosary cried out quarreling, 'Why do you turn me round and round?' Turn mental rosary should you want a Master guide. Telling beads and counting the turns on fingers, Hollow are such deeds of merit, performed with wandering mind. How can God be found with an insensate mind?"

Kabir says, "When doing all ablutions or purificatory exercises like telling the beads, etc., your mind is not still, what is the good of doing them after all? While you are telling the beads and counting the number of rosary revolutions performed on your fingers, the mind like an unbridled colt is wandering about. All such deeds are, therefore, of no avail. You can meet God through a living Master only when, according to His instructions, you learn to bridle the mind and turn it the other way" (i.e., inward and upward from its usual way of looking at things outward and downward). The practice of concentration and focusing of the mind can be achieved only through Simran as enjoined by a Master Soul and by nothing else.

Kabir Sahib further presses the point. "In vain is the rosary that loosens not the mind knot. A heaven veritable lies in the Master's feet alone. No outer shows are needed, all must be done within. Why lose time with the outside world? I am now engaged in my Lord within."

Simran, as said above, is all a mental or inner process and, as such, a rosary or any other aid cannot be of any use in this behalf. By concentration at the blessed feet of the Master, by implicit faith in His instructions, and by putting them into actual practice, we can attain a stage of perfect bliss. There is no short cut but that of Simran as enjoined by the Master.

The Bible, too, says, "Be ye the doers of the Word and not the hearers only," and then you will enter New Jerusalem.

CONCLUSION

The Naam or Word is within you. This is to be contacted within. The observance of the outer rituals and performance of so-called meritorious deeds cannot be of any help in this matter. While the untold treasure of divinity lies hidden within, we search for it without and so all our efforts go in vain.

Emerson in this connection says, "The human body is a temple of God and, as such, God can only be made manifest from within." The contact between an individual spirit or human soul and the Oversoul is, of course, established by a Master Soul by means of the Sound Current or Word.

Another Saint, Bhika, says: "O Bhika, there is no man starving in this world. Everybody has a diamond of precious value within. They do not know how to withdraw from the body and concentrate the sensory current and transcend the lower chakras in the body (or just analyze oneself from the body). That is why they feel hungry. They have the thing within them, but they know not how to come out of the body to contact it."

The Sound Current or Word is contacted through the medium of Simran, which withdraws the spirit current from the body. When the current comes up to the seat of the soul in the waking state, only then it contacts the Conscious Power working within throughout the whole creation. It will, therefore, appear that Simran or the process of the sweet remembrance of the Word is the stepping stone to contacting the Word within. The first step is, therefore, to do the Simran or repetition of the charged words given by a competent Master, and the second step is, when the soul is withdrawn to its seat in the body at back of the two eyes, it contacts the Word which is called Naam, Shabd, Nad, Akash Bani, Kalma, Sarosha, etc. This Word has two phases: one is of Light and the other of Sound, which the soul experiences when it comes in contact with that Power. He sees the Light of God and hears sweet symphonies of the rapturous strains of the Sound Current going on within which gives its sweetness very sublime and ineffable, so sweet that no words can convey.

Farid, a Muslim Saint, says: "O Lord, there are so many sweet things in the world such as honey, buffalo milk, sugar; but the sweetness that Your Name conveys, O Lord, is far sweeter than all these." It is a subject to be done practically and tasted by the individual self. It is not a matter of routine only, nor of mere talking. It is a matter to be experienced by contact within. Those who have tasted the sweet elixir of it have talked about it in glowing terms.

Once Guru Nanak met Babar, the great King of India, who was taking an intoxicant. He offered it to Guru Nanak who told him, "Babar, this drug that you are taking loses its intoxication, but the intoxication I have by contacting the Word of God is everlasting and cannot be diminished." So it is an interesting subject. Those who have once tasted a bit of it can never forget it. All the world's enjoyments and other things lose their weight and value in their own eyes.

Constant remembrance of the Lord further gives a wakefulness to the man who is engaged in it. Tennyson in his Memoirs gives an instance of his experience of a waking trance he had, which could be interesting to know. He says:

> *A kind of waking trance I have frequently had quite up from boyhood, when I have been all alone. This has generally come upon me through repeating my own name two or three times to myself silently till all at once, as it were out of the intensity of consciousness of individuality, the individuality seemed to dissolve and fade away into boundless being and this not a confused state but the clearest of the clearest, the surest of the surest, the wisest of the wisest, utterly beyond words, where death was a laughable impossibility, the loss of personality (if so it were) seemingly but the only true life. I am ashamed of my feeble description, have I not said the state is utterly beyond words.*

This wakefulness Tennyson had by remembering his own name two or three times, quite calmly; this was, as it were, dipping into his own self, the soul. If we but dip in our source — God — by constant remembrance, losing our own selves into the whole, how much greater consciousness and wakefulness full of intoxication we would have. We can well consider all this. Thank you for your patient hearing.

KIRPAL SINGH

About the Author

Considered by many people who met him in the East and in the West to have been a living example of a true Saint of Spirituality, Kirpal Singh was born in a rural setting in Sayyad Kasran in the Punjab (then in India, now in Pakistan) on February 6, 1894. He followed the career of a civil servant in the government of India, and retired on his own pension in 1947. Following instructions from his Master (Sawan Singh Ji Maharaj, 1858-1948), he founded and directed RUHANI SATSANG. He was commissioned by God and authorized by his Master to carry forward the spiritual work of contacting sincere seekers after God with the WORD (or NAAM). He continued in that capacity until he left the earth plane on August 21, 1974. Elected four times, consecutively and unanimously, as President of the World Fellowship of Religions, he upheld the truth that, though the various religions are different schools of thought, the aim of all religions is one and the same. Kirpal Singh visited the major cities in the United States on the occasions of each of his three world tours: in 1955, in 1963-64, and again in 1972, staying in this country for three months or more, each time. From his intense study at the feet of Sawan Singh Ji Maharaj and from his own personal inner experiences of a spiritual nature, Kirpal Singh was eminently qualified to convey to sincere people everywhere the importance of self knowledge and God realization.

Sant Kirpal Singh Ji with Mildred Prendergast, 1963

Kirpal Singh Ji Maharaj

BOOKS by Kirpal Singh

CROWN OF LIFE
A comparison of the various yogas and their scope, including Surat Shabd Yoga—the disciplined approach to Spirituality. Religious parallels and various modern movements cited. Paperback; 256 pages; index.
ISBN 978-0-942735-77-2

GODMAN
If there is always at least one authorized spiritual guide on earth at any time, what are the characteristics which will enable the honest seeker to distinguish him from those who are not competent? A complete study of the supreme mystics and their hallmarks. 232 pages.
Soft Cover ISBN 978-0-942735-64-2
Hard Cover ISBN 978-0-942735-70-3

A GREAT SAINT: BABA JAIMAL SINGH
His Life and Teachings
A unique biography, tracing the development of one of the most outstanding Saints of modern times. Should be read by every seeker after God for the encouragement it offers. Also included, **A BRIEF LIFE SKETCH OF THE GREAT SAINT, BABA SAWAN SINGH,** the successor of Baba Jaimal Singh. He carried on Baba Ji's work, greatly expanding the Satsang and carrying it across the seas. Paperback; 230 pages; glossary; index.
ISBN 978-0-942735-27-7

THE JAP JI: The Message of Guru Nanak
An extensive explanation of the basic principles taught by Guru Nanak (1469-1539 A.D.) with comparative scriptures cited. Stanzas of the Hymns in English, as well as the original text in phonetic wording. 189 pages; glossary.
Soft Cover ISBN 978-0-942735-81-9
Hard Cover ISBN 978-0-942735-85-7

HIS GRACE LIVES ON
During 17 days in the month of August 1974, preceding His physical departure on August 21st, Kirpal Singh gave 15 darshan talks, mostly in the form of questions and answers, to a small group of His disciples at His ashram in India. These talks have been bound together with the unabridged text from Master Kirpal's address to the Parliament of India and His 1971 afternoon darshan talk, True Meditation. Hard cover and paperback; 17 photos; 203 pages.
Hard cover ISBN 978-0-942735-93-2
Soft cover ISBN 978-0-9764548-3-0

THE LIGHT OF KIRPAL
A collection of 87 talks given from September 1969 to December 1971, containing extensive questions and answers between the Master and western disciples visiting at that time. [A different version of this book was published under the title *Heart to Heart Talks*.] Paperback; 446 pages; 15 photos.   ISBN 978-0-89142-033-0

MORNING TALKS
A transcription of a series of talks given by Sant Kirpal Singh between October 1967 and January 1969. "To give further help and encouragement on the Way, my new book *Morning Talks* will soon be available for general distribution. This book, which covers most aspects of Spirituality, is a God-given textbook to which all initiates should constantly refer, to see how they are measuring up to the standards required for success in their man-making. I cannot stress sufficiently the importance of reading this book, digesting its contents, and then living up to what it contains." —Master Kirpal Singh. Paperback; 258 pages.
                         ISBN 978-0-942735-16-1

NAAM or WORD
"In the beginning was the WORD... and the WORD was God." Quotations from Hindu, Buddhist, Islamic, and Christian sacred writings confirm the universality of this spiritual manifestation of God in religious tradition and mystical practices. Paperback; 335 pages.   ISBN 978-0-942735-94-9

THE NIGHT IS A JUNGLE
A compendium of 14 talks delivered by the author prior to 1972, the first four of which were given in Philadelphia in 1955. The remaining ten talks were delivered in India. All of these transcriptions were checked for their accuracy by Kirpal Singh prior to their compilation in this book. Paperback; 368 pages, with an introduction.   ISBN 978-0-942735-18-5

PRAYER: Its Nature and Technique
Discusses all forms and aspects of prayer, from the most elementary to the ultimate state of "praying without ceasing." Also contains collected prayers from all religious traditions. Paperback and hard cover; 246 pages; including the talk *Simran*.   ISBN 978-0-942735-50-5

SPIRITUALITY: What It Is
Explores the Science of Spirituality. Man has unravelled the mysteries of the starry welkin, sounded the depths of the seas, delved deep into the bowels of the earth, braved the blinding blizzards of snowy Mount Everest, and is now out exploring space so as to establish interplanetary relations, but sad to say, has not found out the mystery of the human soul within him. Paperback; 103 pages plus introductory.   ISBN 978-0-942735-78-9

SPIRITUAL ELIXIR
Collected questions addressed to Kirpal Singh in private correspondence, together with respective answers. Also contains various messages given on special occasions. Paperback; 382 pages; glossary.
ISBN 978-0-942735-02-4

SURAT SHABD YOGA *(Chapter 5 of Crown of Life)*
The Yoga of the Celestial Sound Current. A perfect science, it is free from the drawbacks of other yogic forms. Emphasis is placed on the need for a competent living Master. Paperback, 74 pages.
ISBN 978-0-942735-95-1

THE TEACHINGS OF KIRPAL SINGH
Volume I: The Holy Path; 98 pages.   ISBN 978-0-9764548-0-9
Volume II: Self Introspection/Meditation; 180 pages.
ISBN 978-0-9764548-1-6
Volume III: The New Life; 186 pages   ISBN 978-0-9764548-2-3
Definitive statements from various talks, books and letters by the author, reorganized by topic to illuminate the aspects of self-discipline pertinent to Spirituality. Relevant questions are answered. This collection allows the reader to research by topic.
Three volumes sold as one book; 464 pages   ISBN 978-0-9764548-4-X
Complete set in a single volume   ISBN 978-0-942735-33-8

THE WAY OF THE SAINTS
An encyclopedia of Sant Mat from every point of view. This is a collection of the late Master's short writings from 1949 to 1974. Included is a brief biography of Baba Sawan Singh, the author's Master, plus many pictures. Paperback; 418 pages.
ISBN 978-0-89142-026-2

THE WHEEL OF LIFE & THE MYSTERY OF DEATH
Two books in one volume. The meaning of one's life on earth and the Law of Karma (the law of action and reaction) are examined in the first text; in the following text, the reader is presented with the whys and wherefores of "the great final change called death." Paperback; 293 pages; plus index for the first text; and introduction.
ISBN 978-0-942735-80-2

THE WHEEL OF LIFE
Available in hard cover; 98 pages plus glossary and index
ISBN 978-0-9764548-5-4

THE MYSTERY OF DEATH
Available in hard cover; 125 pages   ISBN 978-0-9764548-6-1

THE THIRD WORLD TOUR OF KIRPAL SINGH
This book was printed directly from the pages of *Sat Sandesh* magazine, the issues from October 1972 through February 1973, which were primarily devoted to Master Kirpal Singh's Third World Tour. 160 pages, 80 black and white pictures.

BOOKLETS BY KIRPAL SINGH

GOD POWER / CHRIST POWER / MASTER POWER
Discusses the ongoing manifestation of the Christ-Power and the temporal nature of the human bodies through which that Power addresses humanity. "Christ existed long before Jesus." Paperback; 32 pages.
ISBN 978-0-942735-04-8

HOW TO DEVELOP RECEPTIVITY
Three Circular Letters (of June 13, 1969; November 5, 1969; and January 27, 1970) concerning the attitudes which must be developed in order to become more spiritually receptive. Paperback; 20 pages.
ISBN 978-0-942735-05-5

MAN! KNOW THYSELF
A talk especially addressed to seekers after Truth. Gives a brief coverage of the essentials of Spirituality and the need for open-minded cautiousness on the part of the careful seeker. Paperback; 30 pages.
ISBN 978-0-942735-06-2

RUHANI SATSANG: Science of Spirituality
Briefly discusses "The Science of the Soul"; "The Practice of Spiritual Discipline"; "Death in Life"; "The Quest for a True Master"; and "Surat Shabd Yoga." Paperback; 36 pages.   ISBN 978-0-942735-03-1

SEVEN PATHS TO PERFECTION
Describes the seven basic requisites enumerated in the prescribed self-introspective diary which aid immeasurably in covering the entire field of ethics, and help to invoke the Divine Mercy. Paperback; 52 pages.
ISBN 978-0-942735-07-9

SIMRAN: The Sweet Remembrance of God
Discusses the process of centering the attention within by repeating the "Original or Basic Names of God" given by a true Master. Paperback; 56 pages.   ISBN 978-0-942735-08-6

THE SPIRITUAL AND KARMIC ASPECTS
OF THE VEGETARIAN DIET
An overview of the vegetarian diet containing a letter from Kirpal Singh on the spiritual aspects, a letter from Sawan Singh on the karmic aspects, and excerpts from various books by Kirpal Singh. Paperback; 58 pages.
ISBN 978-0-942735-47-5

Books, Booklets and Audio-Visual Material of Master Kirpal Singh can be ordered from this address or directly online.
RUHANI SATSANG®
250 "H" St. #50, Blaine, WA 98230-4018 USA
1 (888) 530-1555   Fax (604) 530-9595 (Canada)
E-mail: RuhaniSatsangUSA@gmail.com
www.RuhaniSatsangUSA.org